THE GRANNY'S TEA
POETRY MAGAZINE

ISSUE ONE

LIFE STORIES

CONTENTS

1. Contents
2-3. Editor's welcome - Ellie McDonnell and Emily Milburn
4. Werther's - Ellie McDonnell
5. Artwork on the Balcony - Emily Milburn
6. The life of a rider - Amy Quinn
7. Clayoquot Sounds - Jody Bigfoot
8. Phosphorescence - Al Crow
9. Anxiety Keeper - Anastasia Brown
10. Sydney Raspberry Chocolate - Anastasia Brown
11. Biscuits in Bed - Annie Majin
12. a comedy where 'capitalists-for-survival-purposes' become partners in retail crime. - bethellen777
13. The Kitchen - Catherine Hamilton
14. The art of forgetting - Chloe Rowland
15. Conversing with silence - Chloe Rowland
16. Fisherman's Table - Dan Hughes
17. Fragments - Emma Swailes
18. Chronic - Esther Byrne
19. How do we forgive our parents? - Freya Cook
20. Nostalgic ghost - Hanna Elkaram
21. Tynemouth - H. K. G. Lowery
22. Day 71 - H. K. G. Lowery
23. Spring in Lockdown - Jasmine Sara
24. The side chapel - Julie Kinninmont
25. Midnight Ballerina - Kristin J. Thompson
26. Bait Box Bride - Lauren Griffiths-Cook
27. Since the council took the bench away - Lee Jevon
28. The Walk - Mara
29. "Time Dies" - Matthew Lilley
30. Gift of No Return - Mere
31. Ignorance is Bliss - Milie Fiirgaard
32. I SURVIVED? - Mohammed Omer
33. The Ballet Dancer - Naomi Jones
34. Whichever - Nicholas Bielby
35. Corpse Tree - Owen Seth
36. Shatter - Paul Pavely
37. COWGIRL AT GOLGOTHA - Paul Pickering
38. Hands - Rachel Milburn
39. Insides - Rebecca Wright
40. On a hill in North London - Rosie Georgiou
41. Bury Me Deep - Sarah Cain
42. Doll's House - Trisha Broomfield
43. Etched - Zoe Oz
44-45. Poetry articles by Lucas Murray
46. Thank you

EDITOR'S WELCOME

<u>Ellie McDonnell</u>

Hello lovely readers. My name is Ellie McDonnell and I am a co-editor and the publicist here at The Granny's Tea Poetry Magazine.

I would like to take this opportunity to say one big thank you to every single person who submitted to this issue. The support for this project has been far more than we expected and has been appreciated more than we could ever say. You have certainly kept us busy. Reading all of your poems has been both an honour and a joy, you are a very talented bunch.

When editing for the magazine, I was looking for colourful poetry. I love poetry that jumps off of the page; a good poem to me causes an emotional reaction. From little excited dances at my laptop too a few sneaky tears too, it has certainly been a rollercoaster.

I have enjoyed every second of editing your poetry, even the late nights and early mornings. I think I am in need of a little poetry detox but we'll see how long I last before the pen sneaks into my hand once more. Your poems have left me buzzing with too many ideas to mention. The world of poetry is never-ending and this magazine has been the big push I needed to jump head first into the creative industry.

My advice to any poets wanting to join our little community in the future, is too read the brief carefully and draft, draft, draft. So many great ideas are waiting to be uncovered in drafts.

Finally, welcome to The Granny's Tea community. Grab yourself a big cup of tea, get cosy and enjoy the magazine.

Emily Milburn

Welcome reader, to The Granny's Tea poetry magazine! My name is Emily and I am a co-editor of the magazine.

Initially, the idea of The Granny's Tea was pitched in our 'Pitch to Publication' module at Northumbria University. As emerging poets, the team had previously struggled to publish work. A poetry magazine felt like an efficient way to reach audiences without the competitiveness of the publishing industry. We chose 'Life Stories' as the magazine's debut theme because it is inclusive and open to interpretation.

It was not until the project fully kicked off that a vision began to take form. We expected a maximum of ten submissions from our classmates, and resulted in two hundred and eighty from the public. To say that we have been in shock for the last few weeks is an understatement. As Ellie has already mentioned… thank you. Thank you all for making this possible. Thank you for missing out on that social event to jot down a poem, thank you for skipping that meal to note your biography, thank you for staying up late to finish that email. From the bottom of our hearts, thank you and well done.

In each submission, I was looking at the language and structure. Is it concise? Does it make sense? It is supposed to be so simplistic? Is it meant to make me feel this way? My favourite poems are those that aren't afraid to use language to its capability, those that push the limits of sound, musicality, and explosiveness, to create a sensory experience. My advice for future submissions, is to really push yourself. Play around with language and structure, try and create something that *breathes*. Don't worry about your reader, forget about the politics behind the art, and trust the power of language.

Werther's

Sprinting down the drive
Avoiding little porcelain gnomes,
Passed rows of pansies
Scattered to perfection.
No need to knock,
Just storm in
                "Shoes!"
Remember the cream carpet.
Launching into the ornate sofa
Tracing your finger around each swirl in its pattern,
Your hand inching closer
And closer
To the knick-knack table.
Pen and paper next to the landline,
Spare specs abandoned,
Golden wrappers peeking up from a dish,
Werther's in your grasp.
Swirling your tongue around the sweet
Never to be picked in the corner shop
But always your first choice
When you burst through that door.

One stray sweet
At the bottom of your bag,
Perfectly placed
To remind you of her.

 **Ellie McDonnell**

Biography:
I am Ellie McDonnell, a poet born and raised in Gateshead. Poetry is a relatively new form for my creative brain but something which is quickly becoming addictive. Poetry is my space to write how I feel. I write poems to vent. Some I want nothing to do with the minute my pen leaves the page, others I want to hold close and embrace for a little longer. Werther's is one of those poems, one that I will always keep near. This poem was inspired by the magazine title The Granny's Tea, I am remembering all the small nostalgic details about going to my Granny's house. The small details I wish to never forget. Furthermore, I am co-editor and publicist at The Granny's Tea. This project has pushed me in to a whole new world of poetry, one which I will be exploring for a long time to come.

Artwork on the Balcony

brush strokes on canvas
leaving marks
a beautiful distress to plainness

olive skin soaking in the warmth
a white cotton dress
loosely hugging her body

a gentle kiss from the country wind
carrying runaway seeds from the
harvest around

closed eyes   dark lashes
sleeping
in serenity

piano keys   a distant tune   a soft melody
carries in the air like
whispers

wood chips lazing
on the floor
occasionally sticking to her slippers

a grasshopper approaches
to marvel
at her composition

Emily Milburn

Biography:
My name is Emily Milburn. I am a poet from the Lake District in Cumbria, but I am currently based in Newcastle Upon Tyne. I like to think of myself as an English Breakfast Tea connoisseur and furry feline advocate… I am also the co-editor at The Granny's Tea poetry magazine, a role which has nurtured and enriched my poetic practice. Moving to London at eighteen, and Newcastle Upon Tyne at twenty, my poetry swiftly adapted to urban life, discussing themes of displacement, location, nostalgia, and relationships. Artwork on the Balcony is a rare poem of mine, as it focusses on the calmness of country life. The poem visits a moment in time; a woman painting on the balcony as the harvest season flourishes around her. Growing up in the country, this poem warms my heart and comforts me in times of city-life mania.

The life of a rider

The life of a rider
brisk and damp
to go everywhere
and nowhere

the tarmac never ending
my muscles ache
as the vibration hums
through my rib cage

the orange gleam rises
as the horizon stretches
and the rhythm echoes
the melody
pounding
pounding
pounding

wind brushing leather
cold to the touch
and a tingle in my fingers
choking on that biting breeze

I realise now
that the world is much wider
and I wouldn't change
the life of a rider

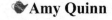**Amy Quinn**

Biography:
Hello! My name is Amy Quinn and I'm a Northumbria student with a mild KISS obsession from South Shields. I love thrilling activities such as motorbike riding, bungee jumping and sky diving, this is something that influences a lot of my poetry. An activity that I would love to check off my bucket list is to fight someone in a sumo wrestling suit and as much as I love the UK, I would love to travel. I've always been completely mesmerised by thunderstorms and would love to visit Lake Maracaibo so that I can write about them at their peak. The main thing to know about me is that I'm a hopeless romantic at heart and this is what I love to write about the most. Last but not least, my biggest claim to fame is that somewhere online, there is a picture of me with Prince William.

Clayoquot sounds

Way ahead of the main spawn, a couple came upstream
To bake in the summer sun whilst smoke smothered the sky.
Inconsistent temperatures left these chinook confused.
One watched the other shed chunks of flesh, half dead, half alive.

The bridge we braved, that fell apart under foot
Was lost to winter storms. We were the last people
To ever cross that dangerously deep ravine.
As it crumbled and my boot fell through, its demise was forewarned

An ancient tree, so big it could hide an elk,
And it did. The biggest beast I've ever seen with my own two eyes.
I'm not sure who was more surprised as I appeared beneath its chin
It turned and fled, though if it attacked I'd surely die.

I used to chase the bears away, shouting with a stick.
I was told that the year before, one got too friendly, and was often around.
No longer scared of humans, it ate the grease from the mechanic's workshop.
Its face so deformed from mechanical fat, they had to put it down.

I rode a horse through the mossy megalithic trees
With a Finnish lapphund in my jacket.
Horses that hid from the rain in a giant stump,
A tree stump big enough for three horses, can you imagine?

To think that I couldn't go back to this rainforest,
Just because I washed my passport.
In my Japanese jeans with far too many pockets to check
I'm still there in my dreams. I stay filled with forested thoughts.

 **Jody Bigfoot**

Biography:
Jody Bigfoot is an anomaly and a renegade in life and in art. He has written and recorded over 100 rap songs, recently culminating in a one hour music video project filmed in Japan called "Duszt". The movie was funded, directed, edited and produced by himself with the assistance of one cameraman and a music producer. Following this, Jody was awarded the DYCP arts grant to learn narrative structure and creative writing moving forward. Since falling in love with honing this craft he has been studying creative writing at Northumbria University. It has been somewhat an endeavour for him to write poetry without a beat and above is one small success moving forward in this new format. A snapshot of one of his many adventures in living and working around the world, these particular moments drawn from a summer working in an ancient Canadian rainforest.

Phosphorescence

There's a bloom of phosphorescence in a poem
that has found its way onto my twitter feed.
The writer describes how fear then terror
helps these tiny organisms shine and I'm taken with this image,
as I sit at the side in the trampoline park.
My girls have just gone into the dodge ball court,
behind the line of breastfeeding mums,
where a pair of teenagers in crop tops and baggy pants
are dealing out brutal lessons in kindness.
There are lawless toddlers in amongst it all,
as well as an unfortunate girl wearing headphones,
the weight of difference across her brow.
I wonder if I should say something,
as the squidgy balls are flung around,
various children casualties of the crossfire.
It's wild in there, and I watch and, slowly,
I realise that all these kids will bloom into their futures,
every one of them – this future so stacked with uncertainty.

 Al Crow

Biography:
Al Crow is a winged creature that lives in a dilapidated nest at the brow of an inland cliff. A scavenger of sadness, Crow works across fiction, creative non-fiction and poetry, exploring the climate emergency and human fragility through these mediums. Recent poems can be found in Broken Sleep's The Last Song, Words for Frightened Rabbit, as well as Anthropocene, Dreich, and Popshot magazines. Mad with coffee, Crow will tolerate tea as long as it is served after midday, with milk and accompanied with a platter of biscuits. Cake is permitted. Never should there be sugar in a drink. Truth is universal.

Anxiety Keeper

I didn't mean to break the COVID laws
I once was reported missing at Scotland Yard
Kissed every boy from brunette to green-haired
Needed to have the time of my life after I
Turned 20
I've opened up
My friends love me and
I'm sleeping under the lounge room

I'm strumming his guitar on the tube
I'm eating birthday cake in winter,
Jumping on the softest sofa in the room
And I'm having drinks 'n dinners on the
West End
14-year-old me couldn't even comprehend
How to do that
How to even face the fear and leave her booming house
Young star, look at you now
You made a dream come true
They keep saying it, you truly believe they're proud of you
I now know that feeling doesn't have to stay the same
Brains change and so did I
I don't want to leave, I've got every excuse not to
So I'll remember London 'til I die

I'm going to the movies in a pink suit
I'm not taking this one for granted
I'm going to the theatre to live out my pursuit
I'm not taking this one for granted

Brains change and so did I
I don't want to leave, I've got every excuse not to
So I'll remember London 'til I die

Anastasia Brown

Sydney Raspberry Chocolate

Grand Maison, a wood fire
Velveteen chocolate
A raspberry cake
Whippets crowded 'round to glow and dust away
English garden on the back river in spring
It was years of country roads
The smell of logs on the fire; chocolate promises
Never before had the night been
Starry and enchanting
Pungent unsung melodies in the garden of love
I was happy whilst it was still dreary
Isn't that a funny thing?

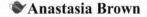**Anastasia Brown**

Biography:
Anastasia Brown is an Australian-born, UK-based writer and filmmaker, with many artistic inspirations directing her work. Growing up in Sydney and moving to London at 19, she is studying a Bachelor in English and Film, gaining inspiration and eduction from British and European forms of literature, media, art + its history. Her experience lies in screenwriting, feminist film + literature, as well as retro cinema. Since March 2020, she has written, run, and managed her review blog 'Dreams of the Screen' and feminist crime-drama noir short film 'The Name Has A Price'. Two of Brown's poetry portfolio works titled 'I Adore My City' (2021) & 'The Peace Piece' (2023) are also in production, set to be self-published. To convey the grand emotion, expression, and potential that both stories and artistic cinema hold is her inspiration.

Biscuits in Bed

I loved you like biscuits in bed –
it was sweet but it crumbled
and burrowed between my sheets,
I swept and shook and clawed
and then I couldn't sleep.
I regret you like biscuits in bed.

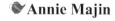**Annie Majin**

Biography:
Annie Majin is a twenty-year-old writer and musician from Kent, currently studying writing at the Royal Central School of Speech and Drama. From a young age, Annie has used poetry to create beauty from misfortune, and hopes to create work that provides people with comfort and peace. Taking inspiration from philosophy, relationships and the changing ways in which love shows itself to us, Annie likes to explore the human condition in a hopeful way. Annie wrote 'Biscuits in Bed' a few years ago while attempting to sleep on a sheet covered in crumbs. The poem serves as a cautionary tale. (She still eats biscuits in bed though.) Annie is also a singer specialising in vintage jazz and swing music; She believes that lyrics are magic and that songs are like confessions. Her favourite song is "11:60pm". Instagram: annie.majin

a comedy where 'capitalists-for-survival-purposes' become partners in retail crime.

i am on the tills
for a floor that
i am not meant to be on.
beg him to wait for me,

we 'leave' without 'permission'.

the next times we meet,
our hands motion warnings
of rain that starts falling.
it's story-time.

no stories are insightful or

mildly important lessons of
my life eats up the minutes,
along with looks of confusion
and hypothetical giggles,

breaking free of ourselves.

of the day, of the job,
of the jobs of the day and the day-jobs,
to do so, we bitch about people quietly -
it's when you said you're proud of me -

or when you say

we
are the keepers of a zoo
with no enclosures.

our wildlife runs too free,

keeping us observant to the chaos,
making our wills to live invisible,
until one of us tries to be funny.
he always reminds me,

just think about the money.

🕊bethellen777

Biography:
I'm Beth-Ellen, a queer creative from London. This is a spoken word piece in which the title is a reference to Capricorns and Scorpios being called 'partners in crime', and how 'retail therapy' is a fun activity, but working in retail is like being in prison. At work, I was getting tired of meeting new people. I felt like I wasn't 'making friends right', until I connected with my scorpio friend. It's the little things, like hiding in fitting rooms or comparing the high street to a zoo, that make the hours pass quickly. Comedy is our silent agreement to get us through the shift. This poem is content in the knowledge that it's connection and interaction that make jobs feel less like chores. It honours a relationship with a coworker, and speaks to conversations that wouldn't make sense to anyone else.

The Kitchen

Laying floor tiles with rubber hammers
Parties with tequila slammers
Counter tops with decks spinning
Dancers grinning
Music blaring
In the morning neighbours staring
Half-filled cans full of fag ash
Lines to the loo with rolled up cash
Singing into kitchen whisks
Beers stains on my compact discs
Hot knives, risky lives, stolen kisses, high fives
Broken biscuit conversations
Drunken late-night declarations
Group hugs, black ties, broken hearts, last goodbyes
Smashed glasses, cracked plates, in a flash safety gates
Cupboards emptied, locks put on
Pictures on the fridge in crayon
First steps to sure footer
Plastic hammers 'fix' the cooker
Ride on bikes slammed into doors
Meals I cooked thrown on the floor
Fun-filled family dinners
Congratulating games night winners
Cupcake baking, mocktail making
Crying into the washing up
When did I become a grown up?
Full of laughter, full of tears
Constantly suppressing fears
So much life, so many goings on
But right now.. kettle on.

❤Catherine Hamilton

Biography:
Catherine Hamilton lives in South London where she loves to watch the birds in her garden. She has been writing poetry since she was a teenager, but still hesitates to call herself a poet. She writes about motherhood, growing up and everything in between, addressing the hardness of it all, but also the humour. She only started to share her work publicly in 2021. Since then, she has had her poetry published in various zines and anthologies.

The art of forgetting

There was laughter, light
popping candy
pecking my mouth like hungry seagulls
and cartoons
blaring out the telly, brewing tea dancing in the air
It smells different at the weekend

There was jigsaws and board games
paint strokes and stories,
graphite-stained hands-
the sign of a good morning with dad
Weightless and blissfully forgetful

And then there was toothbrushes
mouthwash and mint
sliding off his tongue, as glaciers slip into sea
dad's funny dancing
woven through strained eyes
And wordless conversations

And then there was mum
with divorce rolling off her hollow tongue
as easy as pouring your cheerios
under burning eyes
splitting the house in two, even the air hung heavy
bending and slithering round rooms
Suffocated and wishing for forgetfulness to come

Chloe Rowland

Conversing with silence

i can only seem to write in the bath
chatting to the silence
we get on just fine, sometimes
when I'm doing the talking
rolling waves of steam curling through my hands
melting my body warm and
the water cradling my bones
see, I'm not really alone
I think that's the difference
between winning and losing
to silence
today, I won
today –
i wrote

**Chloe Rowland**

Biography:
Ever since my dad introduced me to writing as a child, it's always been something my hands have been drawn to - almost like muscle memory. All the way through my life so far, writing has been the constant that kept me anchored, from childish Sunday mornings with my dad, journaling as a teenager or writing poetry as a 24-year-old alongside my job in journalism. The overarching theme that underpins my work is the development from childhood to adulthood, funnelled through relationships, parental addiction, identity and loss of innocence. Through my work I shed light on how I view myself, whether that be in relation to others, nature, or indeed my own mind. It's my medicine, really.

Fisherman's Table

When I was on the southern sphere, out there on the bay,
peeping at the peaks of lagoon-kissed tides—
I placed a piece of paper on my tongue
and swallowed.

Soon sand ripples became mighty dunes, out there,
my feet like serpents' bellies on the rise.
Glints of glass peppered the moody moon
as I climbed atop the Fisherman's Table.

On the ledge, I braced the hazy tunnel, the water
calling me into its endless depths.
Cackling deep, a drunk hyena, I took
the plunge, knee first:

crack, squelch, crack and black. There were no
endless depths to say hello, just wet rocks.
Clawing past the dunes, a legless crab,
I returned to
Sanctuary.

Encased in walls with bloody knees
feeling just a little sweeter,
I sat alone in thought
eating slices of cold
pizza.

Biography:
Dan is a content writer by day, and a scribbler of oddball prose by night. Originally from Slough, Dan now lives in North Staffordshire by way of North London. His three-year stint in Wellington, NZ, inspired the poem 'Fisherman's Table.' It's based on a hazy and somewhat psychedelic night looking through the 'Doors of Perception' on the Wellington coast while clambering on the balcony of a popular seafood restaurant. Of course, not every trip goes quite as planned. Dan is a fan of spit & sawdust poetry as well as gritty fiction. His latest spoken word collection 'Verbal Spew' is available for public consumption.

Fragments

I find
fragments of broken
shells in my hand
from distant holidays
where bits of broken things
are a joy to collect
a treasure for the future

I find
fragments of broken
heart in my past
from moments of regret
where one loved and lost
collected in ink
a treasure for the future

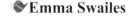**Emma Swailes**

Biography:
Emma is a full-time mum leading a witchy life with her two children. She often uses poetry in magic and creates a successful podcast on being a witch and parenting combined. Although Emma is dyslexic, she has a strong love for reading, poetry and word play. She never lets her bad spelling or fear of ridicule put her off. Emma recently began using poetry as an outlet to keep her mind healthy. For a long time, Emma blocked creativity. To overcome this, she followed The Artists Way 12-week course by Julia Cameron. As a result of her creativity flowing again, the Instagram account @es.poetry.4u was formed. Poetry makes her enormously happy; Emma believes poetry is 'medicine for her mental health'.

<u>Chronic</u>

I am fragile but I fight
Using the exhausted swords in my mind
to fend off threat, both imagined and real

As I gently dream of the amazon I could be –
Standing tall with passion in her soul
Determination etched high and low

I look for the small things –
snatched sunlight peeking through the trees

I am gilded, grey and grateful
Seeing beyond the limited transactions of life
Attaching meaning to the mundane

I have paused but not shut down
I simply have a different lens

There is a storm ahead in my path

I will put on my coat

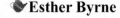 **Esther Byrne**

Biography:
Esther Byrne is a writer from Yorkshire, UK. She has had short stories published with fiftywordstories.com, Toasted Cheese and Secret Attic. In 2021, she was highly commended for the Val Wood Yorkshire prize.
She lives with chronic illness and is passionate about encouraging people with disabilities to express themselves creatively. You can see more of her work at estherbyrne.com and follow her on Twitter, Instagram and Facebook @eshtherbyrnecom.

How do we forgive our parents?

There are hyacinths left in the vase. It's my dad's vase technically-
he bought it from a flea market in Faversham but he's left it behind now.
My mum cannot look at it so I am in charge of these exposed tendrils of nerves.

These ladles of purple,   these tangles of wool-

how easy it is to close your eyes when you are tired.
how easy it is to forget what relies on you.

A memory:
>my mum's favourite carnations for their anniversary.
>the daffodils they bought me after my last exam.
>the lavender in the front garden when they first moved in.

I was not born when they first moved in. I came along later; slipping into the laven-
der bush aged 4 in a game of hide and seek. The sluggish flowers took me into their
arms and welcomed me home and it's hard to talk about home and not talk about the
flowers.

A eulogy:
>the hyacinths died last night. I gave them too much water and I killed them.

These porous-boned streetlights,   these tender-tinted ladders-

how easy it is to hurt something in the name of love.
how easy it is to break something unbreakable by speaking it out loud.

Another eulogy:
>the anniversary carnations. the anniversaries.
>>the exam daffodils. the combined gifts.
>>the garden lavender. the home.

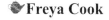**Freya Cook**

Biography:
Freya Cook (she/her) is currently studying English Literature at Durham University. She was commended as a top 100
poet in Foyles Young Poetry competition, was commended in the Young Poets' Keats Challenge, and has been published in
'Ink, Sweat and Tears' and 'The Gentian'. Her work is based on family, loss and home. This poem arose out of her love for
flowers, but her inability to keep any alive! Love is not enough to keep them alive, just as it is not enough to keep a family
together. When not writing, Freya can be found running (very slowly), daydreaming about getting a tattoo but never doing
it, or cross-stitching patterns of Lord of the Rings.

Nostalgic ghost

I want it all: the freedom of a careless mind

the unconditional love of my family, spoiling me every time I visit

the warmth of the Mediterranean sun concealing my face

turning me into a precious golden brown

the freedom in which the only stress worthy

was 'when am I going to see the sea again'

I want to go back: back to the little girl I was

with the full chubby cheeks

where the zimzamat performed

and the girls danced behind the grand tapestries

Where the scent of henna evoked thoughts of happiness and excitement

and tastes of almond and sweet milk

the aunties and aunts of aunties and their aunts laughed and chanted for the newly wedded

girl,

the cousins playing on the quiet streets as to avoid interrupting the practice of girl to wife

I need it all: the excitement, the life, the suns glow, the love,

the constant connection of familiar faces and names

the connection of family and friends,

knowing someone purely from their family name

connection to our history and tradition,

passed on down and sacredly preserved

I need it all, I want it all.

❦**Hanna Elkaram**

Biography:
I am a north east born Libyan who, despite studying STEM subjects at a-level, pursues her passion in literature and poetry while incorporating ideas of identity and diaspora throughout. Alongside my interest of poetry, I have a deep interest in the history of the MENA region prior the Arab spring and how life was back then. Authors and poets who sparked my inspiration to write include Warsan Shire, Hisham Matar and Kaveh Akbar. One day in the future I hope to open a book café and let people enjoy my collection of books because who doesn't love a good book while drinking coffee?

Tynemouth

He smoked hand-rolled cigarettes
& chucked salty chips from Longsands
to seagulls & the King Charles.

The words yet to leave lips. Rockpools,
kelp & crab. There is no time
to sit on the shore, watching water.

Fathered over tobacco & americano,
he said the waters will take you,
shore will always follow storm.

Bench to bin they left, & the tulips
tied for a grandparent wavered
in the brisk sea breeze.

H. K. G. Lowery

Day 71

legs were like lead, gait guilty,
  inching the sun-covered concrete;
the expanse, pavements & empty pubs,
    streets soundless as Zombieland (2009)
& 28 Days Later (2002); his new rule:
    a group of six outside – we bumped elbows,
    mates not separated this long since
                we could speak –
                we were not Chilean minors,
                we were ill at ease & terrible
    skin fades & warm Stella,
exploring our hometown like we would Atlantis,
                        sat outside, distanced,
                        at The Cumberland Arms

♥H. K. G. Lowery

Biography:
H. K. G. Lowery is a writer & musician from Gateshead. He gained a Distinction in his Masters degree in Creative Writing from Graduate College, Lancaster University, where he worked with Paul Muldoon, Terry Eagleton & Paul Farley. The Department of English Literature & Creative Writing awarded him with the 2021/2022 Portfolio Prize for his work which received the highest mark in the faculty. Lowery has been shortlisted for The Bedford International Award & The Terry Kelly Poetry Prize, & his publications include: *An Enquiry into the Delight of Existence and the Sublime* (Austin Macauley Publishers, 2020), *Being and Becoming* (Kindle Direct Publishing, 2021), *Death, And Other Angels* (Errant, 2022) & 9:45 Drama: Selected Poems (Kindle Direct Publishing, 2022). He has been published in *Poetry Salzburg, The Ofi Press, Amsterdam Quarterly, Publishers Weekly, Pennine Platform, Obsessed With Pipework, Dreich Magazine, Train River Publishing, Sylvia Magazine, Lancaster Flash, Errant, Inky Lab Press & NARC Magazine.*

Spring in Lockdown

Spring 2020 sprinkled
freckles across my face,
made no promises and
reminded me to delight in
pink blossom on blue sky.

Fingers loosened their grip
on things out of my control,
finding the threads of stories
longing to be told.

Cold sea water shocked
me awake from stagnation,
redirecting droplets of doubt
to seeds of creation.

❤ **Jasmine Sara**

Biography:
Jas is a writer from the Newcastle Upon Tyne. She's lived, worked and studied all around the world, collecting stories along the way. Her poetry is often personal, capturing moments in time as a way to process and remember life experiences. She runs an ethical design and copywriting studio called Ardea Creative, and is learning all the time about how to make space for her own creative practice alongside running a business.

The side chapel

(Trigger Warning: Shocking imagery)

She was so innocent
Still skipping in the lanes
When they laughed "you won't be doing that much longer"

She only understood weeks later
Abdomen taut
Shame and fear lurking behind each net curtain
The wedding was hurried, hushed
The side chapel

Even years later
Cradling her fourteenth
Body rich and raw once again
She couldn't forget the sting of it
They'd only let her use
The side chapel

**Julie Kinninmont**

Biography:
Julie (@_jules_writes_) writes heartfelt, thoughtful and sometimes quirky poetry about mental health, relationships, identity and being human. She has been published in a number of zines and literary journals including MIDLDMAG, Strawberry, ItsOK, OnTheHigh and Bi Women Quarterly. Her work has been showcased at open mics and literary festivals and she loves making connections with other creatives. When she's not writing over a huge mug of tea, she enjoys performing improv, having a cider at a festival, or faffing about with a hula hoop. You can find more of her work at bit.ly/juleswrites or come see her perform at a poetry night near you!

Midnight Ballerina

I'm reading Seidel at the cabaret
Luna moth amongst Chanel and powdered tables thinking about a shotgun and a
pointing dog.
I don't really belong here
but I most definitely do not belong anywhere else.

I'm the monster of the modern renaissance
plagued with a choice but no voice,
smiling in sparkling stilettos and scribbling about
my complicated relationships with my father and God,

dancing for strangers in hopes
that a few will take pity on me
though I'd torch the whole business
for a good read and some
genuine company.

They all want to know if I am happy.
They all know that I will lie,
but,
they still ask me.

❦Kristin J. Thompson

Biography:
Kristin J. Thompson is a literary and visual artist, the author of 4 books of poetry, and the co-founder of an indie academic
press called Back of the Class Press. She also owns a photography and poetry magazine named MyrtleHaus Magazine and
works professionally as an anthropologist and archaeologist. Kristin has spent the last three summers studying in Europe
and is working in Greece excavating an ancient ruin this summer. In her spare time, you can find her hosting film classes,
creating tintypes, reading with her cat, raising moths, digging up bones overseas, and curating art collectives. Her work can
be viewed online at kristinjthompson.com.

Bait Box Bride

I was born to be a bait box bride,
when the boys went by always smiled.
They made sure I could count to a dozen,
bake a nice sponge, and stitch up a button.

I fell for a ring and a grin and grew wide,
now every day is baked, boiled, or fried,
smoked or braised, never brazen or cutting,
homely and comely, lamb dressed as mutton.

Two little lads made of stone barrel home, eat me whole.
Again the nest's feathered, my mother had seven, can't moan.
Takes my breath, the strength from my bones, leaves us wilting,
wear me down til my sole aspirations a sit in

'Tween adorations, congratulations, and exhortations
from conglomerations of unwelcome visitations
libations fuel insinuations,
they call your father young'n.

They're so sure their bairn, rough hewer, just as poor
will take her up the church on the moor, knee deep in manure
with nee inclination to woo her
'fore he pulls generations of these village nations through her.

Yet hyphenation initiates apron liberation,
your double barrels a weapon for gutting these gluttons
who'd incacerate you for a shut in,
their fortifications the weight of a pin cushion

Had my dad turned the sands, planned my hand 'fore i could stand?
Warden to warden, a change of address only remand
hide the hopes and dreams, my contraband,
no brand for your hide, no shuttered eyes, I'll bear the backhand

Take this snide little world in your stride, know when you watch the distant tides,
I couldn't have mired my child inside these aberrations, the dead eyed lives of bait box
brides.

❦Lauren Griffiths-Cook

Biography:
Hello, I'm Lauren, a Durham-born poet and author unsurprisingly obsessed with the pit. I'm usually a prose writer off
exploring other worlds, but I always feel the call to write about real life in the North East. The lives of men in my family
history have always been a great source of inspiration for me, but their wives seemed so quiet in those stories that got told
at family parties. It was like they stopped existing while their husbands were under the clarts. With this poem I wanted to
fight back against that narrative of the neatly packaged housewife and mother, break the cycle of thinking of these women
like that and writing them hovering at the window.

Since the council took the bench away

Where mums no longer stop to chat,
pigeons gather now
as crowds, drawn
to scenes of great disaster.

Memories, once entwined with wooden slats,
of teenage dreams explored through fumbled lust,
lay fallen at the doors of shut-up shops, or
etched on wooden windows -
since the council took the bench away.

Dog walkers need not fear the sleeping men,
whose empty cans of comfort tell a tale,
of choices made and consequence.

In battered armchairs old folk reminisce
alone and not as one.
Not like before
Since the council took the bench away.

Lee Jevon

Biography:
Lee discovered his passion for writing as a youngster, finding that it could unlock the imagination and create new outlooks on the world. His poetry focuses on the world we live in and is at once, exploratory, judgmental and hopeful. He has been a self-employed writer for seventeen years and, after graduating with a masters degree in creative writing in 2019, has returned to his love of writing poetry.
In his day job, as well as writing comedy sketches and one-liners that have featured on BBC radio and TV, and on TikTok he has written extensively on finance, entertainment and sport. He's even turned his hand to all sorts of bogs and articles - including how to remove stains from a toilet bowl!

The Walk

We walked back together,
The night wrapped around us,
Thick and balmy, like silk.
We were wrapped in each other
The only people in the world.
Hands hands hands -
Desperate lips on lips,
And neck and cheek and collarbone -

We flared red in the inky blue,
The street swirled around us,
Quiet as a stage.
The buildings whispered back,
A gift of soft laughs and quiet moans.

We walked back together.
The walk seemed endless
To you,
But with you wrapped around my waist
Urgent and alive behind me
I could have walked forever.

Mara

Biography:
I am a twenty-something closet poet writing through the glorious messiness of learning how to live a life for myself, and only myself, in London. My poetry has long been a carefully guarded secret in the 'Notes' app on my phone, a loyal confidante for moments of joy and ugliness alike; but after tentatively sending this poem to a friend nine months ago, I find myself wanting to share it with you, reader. I wrote this after a night that stuck in my mind for months afterwards, the kind of night that is exactly what you want and need it to be. I want my poetry to make you feel something – whether it's what I felt at the time, or something entirely different. Poetry is a thing entirely of its own, and I would like nothing more than for this to be as much yours as it is mine.

"Time Dies"

The hearth of my course:
Learning about images,
Bending the mind's hands.

Winged hourglasses
Circle me. Oh, how banal!
I'll work my magic.

My mind forms a gun
That fires written bullets
And shoots their wings out.

My mind forms the tools
To build their grounded bodies
Into a prison.

It fills up with sand.
Is this grain my punishment
For playing with time?

Will it turn back time,
Or bury me in the dunes
Of melancholy?

My mind forms a fist
That punches through time's glass bars
And the sand follows.

It is swept away;
The winds blow towards the east.
Clocks are compasses.

I follow the hands
Away from my mind's device,
But I go slowly.

❦Matthew Lilley

Biography:
One thing that you should know about me is that I often look back to the past.
I graduated with a BA in English Literature and Creative Writing from Northumbria University in 2022. One of the biggest things that I took away from my degree is the knowhow to create new images, or to re-invent old ones.
"Time Dies" is a series of haikus about looking back to the past, no matter how recent or how distant it is, and forwards to the future. I wanted to write something involving winged hourglasses, but coincidentally, that image is the most common literal representation of "time flies." I looked back to my degree and thought about how to re-invent the image. Theme and structure were important to me, but my priority was to be original with my imagery, and to have fun doing so.

Gift of No Return

(Trigger Warning: Domestic violence)

You gave to me the gift, passed down to you
Wrapped inside your mother's sari
Something deeper than love, heavier than sadness
The tears of her sister broken by drunk hands, a violent man
A well of warmth, folded neatly in the parcel of banana leaves
The spool of silk, that led us across the ocean
The blade the empire used to split us from our mother (still sharp enough to cut you)
      and one small gift, you dig from inside your heart
the space to heal what you could not

Mere

Biography:
Mere is a poet and writer based in the North West. Her poetry explores themes of identity, memory, grief, and healing, and the relationship between the past and present. Her work blends the autobiographical with the surreal. She is working on her first collection. Outside of poetry, she is a writer, researcher and advocate for social justice and health equity.
Gift of No Return unpicks the complexities of what we inherit from our families, the love, strength, and wounds passed down – the parts unspoken yet ever present. In imagining the invisible as material, the piece calls attention to the richness and weight of cultural heritage and acknowledges that the two cannot be untangled. Gift of No Return considers the strength of the women before her and how our identity is shaped by the lived experiences of previous generations.

Ignorance is Bliss

Now, half past six you dig out the rum
That you had saved for your sister's wedding
Last year. You smile and crown yourself as king –
I laugh and agree… "I spoke to my mum
Last week," I say. Face falls, I bite my thumb.
"Later," you answer – I think your drinking
Is dulling the surprise. I cannot bring
Myself to repeat; we both come undone.
I wish we could discuss what she said,
If only my worry was unfounded.
But I swallow the thought this weekend
And bask in your light that has blinded
Me completely. By nearly sunset
The bottle is broken, but I am mended.

♥**Milie Fiirgaard**

Biography:
I'm one of those neurodivergent people who know a little about a lot after spending hours hyperfixating on a new hobby or researching random topics. I'll spend 5 hours making one Christmas card, listening to music - it's my form of meditation. That's probably how my passion for writing began too. I remember when my English teacher caught me zoning out in class, scribbling a poem about my dad. She didn't tell me off; instead, she told my mom that the poem was part of my homework and asked me to write her another. I wrote her more than one. My passion for language has only grown, leading me to lots of travels and new words. After living in South Korea, I got my BA in English from Copenhagen University and did my MA in Creative Writing and Publishing at Bournemouth University. I also have poems in Fresher Publishing's anthology Cutting It Short.

I SURVIVED?

The war ended, and I survived,
Two lies to disguise the sacrifice,
Of being told that I made it home,
Even though I am not whole,
A part of my soul fell behind,
Traumatised and abandoned,
How did I survive?

All died longing for home,
We saw death and blood,
The horrors of fear and hate,
A sacrifice that we did not control,
A life we did not own,
We were forced to fight,
And to kill at first sight.

Memories embedded in our minds,
Are those of which we cannot escape,
The meadows barren of life,
All of nature's beauty erased,
The peace replaced with rage,
The trenches and blood,
Is all that remained.

Mohammed Omer

Biography:
The piece "I Survived?" is focused around the painful truths of conflict. We rarely understand what conflict means; this piece is written to help understand the loss involved in war. Both the human loss and the loss in the natural world. There is always physical and mental trauma involved in conflicts. In many cases, life pays the ultimate price with suffering in every way imaginable. Friends and family never returning, nature destroyed in the process. Mohammed is a writer from Manchester. He explores a wide range of topics in his poetry, expressing and experimenting with different styles. He endeavours to raise awareness for important issues in society and wildlife, by using his unique perception to share different perspectives. He has been published by Scribbles (E-zine) and the Ink Pantry. His work can be found on LinkedIn and Instagram.

The Ballet Dancer

An old man now,
with sore, stiff fingers,
a gruff laugh,
a wild grey beard,
he even peers over his spectacles
but
there is still something in the way he sits,
the straight back,
chin held up
that hints at who he was before.

**Naomi Jones**

Biography:
Naomi Jones is a poet, children's author and freelance editor. Her published picture books include The Perfect Fit, One More Try, The Odd Fish, How to Catch a Rainbow, How to Make a Story and Thunderboots. Her picture books have now been translated into 19 languages. Naomi's poem The Ballet Dancer is about her Uncle – he was a farmer's son who was invited to train for the Royal Ballet in London. He went on to dance as a lead dancer for Sadler's Wells Royal Ballet before breaking his back on stage during a performance. After that he taught ballet all over the world. He now lives in Brixham by the sea. Naomi lives with her family and their dog in Cornwall.

Whichever

It's many years since I last dreamt of her.
I dreamt of her last night. I see her in
an airport, leading a Saga group, and turn
to speak to her, thinking, "That's it. Your hair
is different. Cut differently." I touch
her shoulder and I say, "How pretty you look."
Taken by surprise, she turns a cool cheek
for me to kiss, too flustered to say much.

The girl whom I am with has climbed the stairs
And turns to look for me. I have to go.
And she turns back to her companions too.
Then I remember hearing that she has
divorced and got remarried recently.
"Perhaps," I think, "that could, once, have been me."

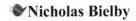**Nicholas Bielby**

Biography:
After retiring from Leeds University School of Education in the last century, Nicholas Bielby became editor of the poetry magazine Pennine Platform for fifteen years. In 2008, he started Graft Poetry, initially to publish poetry books for people whom, from their track record in Pennine Platform, he felt deserved book publication. He has himself written six books of poetry, four academic books, and has contributed to others and to educational journalism. He has won prizes in several poetry competitions including the Arvon International and New Poetry. Born in 1939, he went from grammar school in Huddersfield to read English under F R Leavis in Cambridge, but swapped to philosophy after two years. Subsequently he lectured in Agra University in India, and taught in Nigeria and in special education and Primary education in England, before moving into teacher education. He is married, with two children and three granddaughters.

Corpse Tree

(Trigger Warning: Distressing imagery)

When I die
When the machine runs out of juice
Because of murder
Or malfunction
Or poor upkeep
(Probably poor upkeep)
Stuff me inside an egg
A Papier-mâché pod, I think
That's what I want
Not for anyone else to waste time on wicker boxes
Or wooden caskets
Or burying or burning or even shooting me out of a bloody cannon!
Just break my legs
Bend my arms
Snap my back
Fold me like a jacket
And stuff me into that pod
That's filled with arboreal embryos
So that reincarnation can be given a chance to prove itself
Because we all dissolve in the end
Swallowed up by the cycle of life
Might as well try to live on somehow
As that corpse tree
On that hill over there
Just beyond the church
Watching over a field
Where dead men lie

**Owen Seth**

Biography:
Owen Seth is an aspiring author and poet hurtling towards middle-age. Occasional grappler of both men and words, he lives in the Northeast of England with his wife and their stripey cat, surrounded by good friends, good bars and the smell of fresh fish.
His work traverses the liminal spaces between subjective and objective meaning and the human need for something to work towards. Corpse Tree is about contemplating one's own death and how that in death one may still be able to give back to the world, regardless of how much they took from it in life.

<u>Shatter</u>

When I was a child
if something was too hot
or too sharp I'd drop it
or jump back.

As I grew older, I taught
myself how to hold on
to the pain
until I could find a safe
place to set it down.

Better to suffer than to,
in reacting instinctively,
break something or
harm someone else.

Now I'm learning that sometimes,
there is no safe place.
That it's better to just let go
and trust that not
everything dropped
shatters.

Paul Paveley

Biography:
Paul is a poet, Trekkie and late diagnosed autist from Birmingham. He started writing in his early thirties because it was cheaper than therapy. He started sharing his writing due to the belief that in being brave enough to be vulnerable we give each other permission to do the same. In his writing he intends to attempt to explore themes such as class, mental health and autism, but mostly just ends up writing letters to himself about times he was sad.
His poem "Pocket Fluff" was recently published in The Thicket magazine.
In his spare time, you'll likely find him pedalling around in skin tight lycra, because he felt calling himself a poet was making him too popular.

COWGIRL AT GOLGOTHA

She sucked in each breath passionately,
Her body obeying a solemn duty
Even though her mind had slipped away,
Some two hours before, in this care home Golgotha,
That saw her pressed against candy-stripe pillows
Gasping her last contact with her narrowed world
Like Our Lord did on the cross, before the vinegar,
And the spear in his side, to discover
If life still pulsed in his nerves and veins and muscles,
For it is important to cling like a seaside limpet
To every last moment of the blood and sweat physical,
Even when it is painful to open one purple eye,
Pierced and puffed by a crown of bitter thorns.

My mother's body was keeping this bleak faith
In a small room plastered with photographs,
But another part of her was furiously riding
A range without measure, in splendored sunset glory.

Secretly, she always wanted to be a cowgirl.

❦Paul Pickering

Biography:
I have written seven novels, *Wild About Harry, Perfect English, The Blue Gate of Babylon, Charlie Peace, The Leopard's Wife & Over the Rainbow and Elephant. The Blue Gate of Babylon* was a New York Times notable book of the year, "Superior literature", and I was chosen as one of the top ten young British novelists by bookseller WHSmith and have been long-listed for the Booker three times. As well as writing short stories and poetry I have written several plays, including *Coming Home at the Playground Theatre, "Fury and fun," & Stephen Fry*, and have just finished a new play. I also have a doctorate in Creative Writing from Bath Spa University where I am a Visiting Fellow. Best of all J.G. Ballard described my work as "truly subversive".

Hands

You hold their hands for such a short time.
Constantly worried, anxious, afraid for them.
Small hands that are all encompassed by your own;
for safety, for comfort, to encourage to inspire.
You yearn for them to be independent, to go it alone.
The growth becomes rapid and panic sets in.
They can cross the road alone, hold a pen, brush their own hair.
The need is less now, I am not sure I like it.
Fear takes hold, I am not ready.
Hands that create-that express so much more.
Those hands take a steering wheel, complete exams, apply makeup.
Those sticky fingers now constantly tapping on phone screens.
They no longer need help with that jigsaw, or someone to take the top from the glue.
They read to themselves, silently, no longer animated. Rhyme is no longer needed.
Novels are devoured in the quiet, thick of night, they read to learn, for pleasure.
Now they pack boxes and uni beckons, Gap years and new chapters.
I will watch from afar; they struggle and grapple and strive alone.
They will wipe their own tears now, deal with so much more alone.
I am still here, longing, pining, hungry for news, to smell them, to touch them.
No longer a priority, life is hectic, visits are few. Calls are hurried.
'You have done a good job, they are independent'.
I will always crave to hold their hands once more.

❦Rachel Milburn

Biography:
Hi, my name is Rachel. I am a farmer from Cumbria and do not have much experience in the creative industry. When I first saw the open call for The Granny's Tea online, it was one of my daughters that encouraged me to create something, and submit. I must confess that writing poetry did not feel natural at first; I felt vulnerable and I did not enjoy the feeling. But over the past few days, I have really thrown myself in the deep end, with the hopes of trying something new. I've found that poetry has the ability to connect people, places, and things. In this poem, I feel connected to my growing daughters through verse.

Insides

I have been housing two consciences since the May before last. Two livelihoods
gripping for hold of the mic, pulling away from the meeting point.
Walking in twos like animals onboard the ark,

the sea just as turbulent. The salt-spit just as rancid on my tongue.
My head swells and ripples to home
double the thoughts.

I look for the numbers he leaves me. I search, for longer than I'd care to admit.

I try to do him justice, to say
what I think it is he wants.
Though I am not sure which voice is which anymore.

Who is it that answers the door, that picks up the phone,
that hugs my brother just a little tighter than I used to?

My heart is clogged with promises I pinkie-swore to keep.

As my arms wrap themselves around our ribcage, I know
that the hug I am giving myself is not entirely mine.

It feels so red, so internal,
"Why is grief synonymous with blue?" I ask the air
I doubt he knows either.

❦**Rebecca Wright**

Biography:
Hi, my name is Rebecca and I'm a 21-year-old poet based in the North-East! I'm currently studying my Undergraduate
degree in English Literature at Newcastle University, and I love to write in my spare time. A particular focus in my writing
is unpacking the relationships between people, and analysing the connections we make with others. I think that our rela-
tionships to others are so important, none of which should be taken for granted - from the barista at your local coffee shop,
to your soulmate(s)! I lost my dad right after I turned 19, so a couple of my poems centre around grief, loss and the idea of
'carrying' someone's memory with you after they've gone. I believe the relationships we build with others outlast us all,
and we should all be more grateful for those around us.

On a hill in North London

rests a concrete magpie's nest. Petite, posh.
The sun shoots rays through the lattice window,
and motley figures dance on the cream wall.
Blushing stones link arms with royal blues on
a sandy crest. This is a ball for gems.
Finally he brings out to me, roses:
'These were grown in oysters some years ago.'
Rolling violently on velvety pink
ocean tongues. Moon-pearls cradled in hard gold
petals bloom out from the stems in my ears.
Your fingers trace the soft flesh of my lobes,
your warm breath, a plume sweeping my shoulders.

Love fades. Rain falls. Tender hearts are broken.
Buy these for me, let me keep this token.

❤Rosie Georgiou

Biography:
Rosie Georgiou is a teacher, writer and Creative Writing PhD student living on the east coast of Essex. She is currently researching the ways in which fourth wave feminist politics interact with 1990s British chick lit and the potential innovations in literary form that might emerge from this at De Montfort University. Inspired by themes of nature and memory, her poetry is understood by feelings of nostalgia. She is currently working on her first novel.

Bury Me Deep

(Trigger Warning: This poem contains material relating to child loss.)

Lay me to this solemn ground
Let the roots of my hair take hold
Fragile strands nourished by the fungus
That guide me to where your soft head rests
I wrap around you a thousand times
And a thousand times more
Just to feel you close.

As nitrogen poisons my grieving heart
I grasp at the soils we both now feed
Losing myself again, to you, for you
Tears fill tiny pockets of air
And I am close to sleep
Dreaming, waiting
To be with you anew.

Still we lie, as the cold hours pass
Entwined, our bodies bound
With maternal love
Unending love
Love forced into the ground
Without understanding –
Never to be wrenched free.

❦**Sarah Cain**

Biography:
Sarah Cain is a teaching assistant and mum of four from Harrogate, North Yorkshire. She has been writing poetry for about two years on various themes based around family and nature. Her poem 'Bury Me Deep' is a tribute to her son Ollie, who passed away shortly after birth. She says "Those first few months after loss are very raw and emotional". This poem shares some of the intense feelings she experienced at this difficult time. Some of her other work has appeared in the York Literary Review (2022), Hope is a Group Project (Wee Sparrow Poetry Press, 2022), Scran : Issue 1 (2022), Celebrate (5th Ripon Poetry Festival 2022) and Sleep: Issue 3 (Swim Press 2022).

Doll's House

I make curtains, daisy prints, white on brown,
smiley orange centres. I hem by hand,
string them on wire, tongue out, childlike.
I paint cupboards, bamboo and white,
drawers too, avoiding drips; spills on pebble vinyl.
I buy covers, red stretched, for pre-loved chairs
with threadbare arms.
A Welsh dresser guards a soup tureen, bowls and plates,
country scenes in brown and green.
I soften the dark wood table with chenille,
plant an ironing board, and carpet sweeper.
I sit and knit to the sound of silence.
You, seeing that our house is picture perfect,
satisfied that I fit the wifely bill,
resume your single life,
the sharp edge of the knife,
while I, blinkered, sweep the floor,
paint over more,
in the doll's house of my own design.

🖤Trisha Broomfield

Biography:
My name is Trisha Broomfield, I write daily, I can't help myself. Recently I joined with Sharron Green and Heather Moulson to form, The Booming Lovelies, to perform and also to teach poetry forms at a The Solar Sisters in Guildford. I read monthly at the Solar Sisters and record for poetry podcast, Poetry Worth hearing. I read at an open mic night locally too. The emphasis is mostly on humour, again I can't help it, but some serious poems escape. My poems appear monthly in a local magazine and during Lockdown I had a regular slot on our local radio. I have had three poetry pamphlets published by Dempsey and Windle and featured in many anthologies, including *Poems for Ukraine*, 2022 by Poetry Performance. In 2020 I was short listed for The Arts Richmond Roger McGough Poetry Prize and 2022 long listed in the Plough Poetry Competition.

Etched

I think I want this to be
my last first date

I think the way the water
droplets gently
fall around and splash your boots
as I see you
and the way your umbrella
catches the rain
whilst you're running towards me
somehow stops time
completely for a second
inside my mind

Wonderstruck I stare at you
your dark brown waves
fall softly over blue eyes
that smile at me
like an artwork curated
delicately
for an audience of one

In this moment
in every moment on
all I can see
is you

Zowie Oz

Biography:
I met him for the first time on a rainy day, outside Café Etch in Middlesbrough. He was late and slightly flustered because he'd left his phone at home, and had asked a passing stranger for directions. The entire moment was magical, as though written for a romantic comedy. Opposite the Café, behind him a mural painted with the quote "On me your voice falls as they say love should, Like an enormous yes." by Philip Larkin. I knew already that my heart had been won, and we had the kind of chemistry that saw his 6pm appointment come and go because nothing else existed outside of one another. We eventually became an item, until one day he unexpectedly broke my heart with the news that he was moving to Cambodia for work and was ending the relationship. The last time I saw him was for coffee in Café Etch.

DOES POETRY HELP US HEAL?

Emotions are a constant in our lives. To feel an inescapable reality that we are all subjected to. With pleasure and pain so entwined, sometimes it can be hard to express oneself truly, or even to unpack your feelings at all. This is where poetry can come in; we are able to communicate so much through our craft that mere words are simply not be able to match. Be it overwhelming happiness or crushing sadness, we can feel the release of emotion through poetry, granting oneself a catharsis of sorts, almost as if the emotions are flowing out of us through the ink of our pen. We can lean into the absurd, using abstract poetry to deal with very real problems. Or we can have a uniform structure, with everything clear as day and set in stone – the possibilities are endless, and whatever way you chose to write your poetry remember that it is first and foremost, for you.

WHERE DOES POETRY COME FROM?

Poetry can come from anywhere, anyone and anything. It can come from the smile the cashier gives you as you leave the checkout, which, unbeknownst to them, you really needed today. It can come from your morning walk, as the sunlight hits the canopy of trees that surround you, illuminating their leaves in a way that you hadn't quite noticed before. It can come from something as simple as your kitchen sink, as you are struck with appreciation for the intricacies of the nuts and bolts hidden by the silver casing. Poetry is all around us, always. Sometimes it can be hard to realize, sometimes it can be hard to let yourself feel properly, genuinely and completely. When this happens, take a step back. Take a deep breath. Look around you. Look within you. Take notice. Poetry is everywhere. You just have to look for it.

A POEM CAN TRANSFORM...

Using poetic devices such as a metaphor or a simile can transform the meaning of words on a page, expressing ideas that are otherwise not communicated through simply the idiom used. A poem can use structure to transform its meaning, giving a visual representation to help reinforce its message. Aside from changing itself, poetry can also change lives. Have you ever looked at some words on a page, and felt your entire emotional landscape change? Poetry can move mountains, defeat armies and comfort us in a way we never knew we needed. It is powerful, raw, transformative. Ultimately, it is real. Just like the effects it can have.

OR CAN IT?

By Lucas Murray

FROM EVERYONE AT
THE GRANNY'S TEA
POETRY MAGAZINE

THANK YOU

Printed in Great Britain
by Amazon